MW00856061

STATUS UPDATE

George Toles

Cliff Eyland &

George Toles

Cliff Eyland

AT BAY
press

WINNIPEG

George Toles

Cliff Eyland

George Toles

STATUS UPDATE

Text Copyright © May 2021 George Toles
Illustrations Copyright © May 2021 the Estate of Cliff Eyland

Design by M. C. Joudrey and Matthew Stevens
Layout by Matthew Stevens and M. C. Joudrey

Published by At Bay Press May 2021

Library and Archives Canada cataloguing in publication is available upon request.

ISBN 978-1-988168-37-1

Printed and bound in Canada.

First Edition

10 9 8 7 6 5 4 3 2 1

atbaypress.com

This book is printed on acid free paper that is 100% recycled ancient forest friendly (100% post-consumer recycled).

MIX
Paper from responsible sources
FSC® C016245
FSC www.fsc.org

For Cliff Eyland

November 7, 1954 – May 16, 2020

TABLE of CONTENTS

53 most innocent bystander

54 starlight happiness

55 graveyard

56 attacking his disengagement

57 big family reunion

58 change for the worse

59 santa

60 missing son

61 sea of kindness

62 skeleton guest

63 shit fan

64 hatred beats love

65 shriveled heathens

66 porch steps

67 symbolizing unhappiness

68 self deception

69 near car crash

70 core of dullness

71 potato fame

72 death in bed

73 distant father

74 no forgiveness

75 last night remained

76 tragedy family

77 getting useless advice

78 magic chair

79 fear vs boredom

80 heart or vagina

81 big dinner guest

82 divorce

83 singled out

84 party tricks

85 castrated chauffer

86 aunt kremia

87 useless list

88 dream boat

89 sell insurance

90 remarriage

91 ugly knight

92 tortured imagination

93 dad's visit

94 indestructible illusions

95 wedding investigation

96 moment of family happiness

97 second upbringing

98 farewell

99 like a child

INTRODUCTION

"These paltry details are all that will ever be known about Suzanne. She is fated never to appear in another story, even one as small as this. She is lying on the divan now, looking right at you, reader. She bids you a fond farewell." (Status update, pg. 29)

There is an accidental poeticism to the phrase 'status update,' an enticement from Facebook, Inc. to share one's current mood with an assortment of indifferent acquaintances. Unlike 'post,' the contemporary synonym, 'status update' demands something of the writer. It is a perverse invitation to spill one's guts, to leave a digital footprint of one's inner life. Although the endless social media feed creates the strong impression of transience, we are also aware of the peculiar permanence of everything we share online. That tension, between transience and permanence, is always at play in Cliff and George's collaboration.

For over a decade, my father has written and shared at least one piece of creative writing every day as a Facebook status update. These bits of microfiction (or 'penny dreadfuls,' as he once referred to them) are self-contained works. Though they often gesture to larger contexts or narratives, each one exists to be read and understood on its own, complete in its incompleteness. At the same time, the frequency and regularity of the updates elevates and enhances each piece in relation to the others. A melancholy tale of loss is often sharply contrasted the next day by a raunchy punchline. In these abrupt variations, new perspectives are created for each piece: the surrealist hilarity of grief and the tragic loneliness of sex.

Cliff shared George's obsessive artistic productivity and, in a truly Herculean feat of output, provided illustrations for more than a thousand pieces of writing. Their collaboration is, in my view, a perfect blend of mediums. Many of Cliff's illustrations seemed to emerge powerfully, often violently, from his subconscious, expressing vividly strange glimpses of the people, objects, and landscapes that haunt our lives. The drawings explore and expand on the humour, pathos, and empathy of each piece of writing, often highlighting a messy, troubled figure at the center, or zooming in to show a key object in gruesome, Brobdingnagian proportions. Just as George's writing style shifts between updates, so does Cliff's illustration, which includes photography, paintings, line drawings, and purely digital creations, sometimes alienating nods to the backdrop of these works: Facebook's online wasteland.

I hope my selection of a tiny percentage of Cliff and George's works gives an accurate impression of their vast imaginative achievement. Though themes emerge (death, sex, missing mothers and fathers, personal failure), I tried to refrain from giving too much order to the collection, opting instead to preserve the sense of wild spontaneity that George and Cliff have carefully developed. One hopes that, as George noted in an essay on the criticism of V.F. Perkins, "the essence of the world can be extracted from judiciously chosen, intensely felt particles."

Thomas Toles
July 4, 2020
Winnipeg

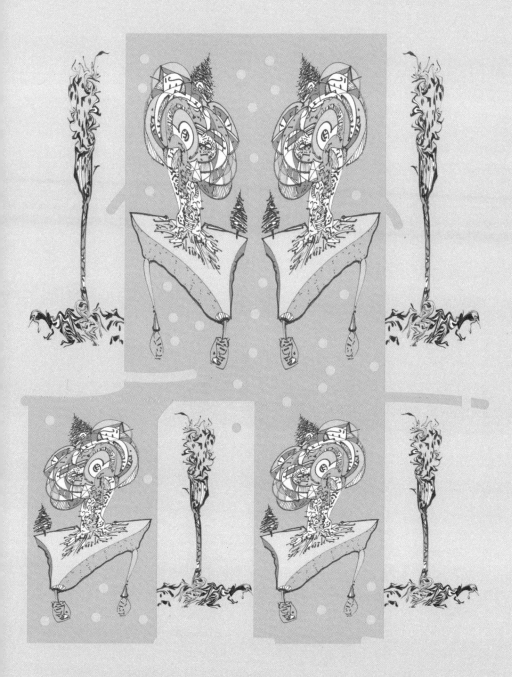

The abandoned children had made themselves into a flower garden of sorts in one of the smaller city parks. Busy passersby tarried, to take a pleasant look. So many plants in human form stretching out their leaves and displaying their blossoms. One scarcely noticed the irregularities in the colorful, well-tended rows. Flowers ask for so little. They have a gift for helping us forget their common destiny.

Status update, 08 July 2011

Mr. Big introduced Laskin to his sons and, in their presence, asked Laskin if he thought they looked like idiots. Laskin knew a lot was riding on his answer. Mr. Big wanted hired killers who were trustworthy and, above all else, truthful. When Mr. Big had earlier asked him whether he thought his wife was good enough for a man of his caliber, he had gulped, closed his eyes, and said "No." That proved to be the correct response. Laskin studied the sons' faces closely and decided that they did look like idiots in most respects. One of them, though, was toting an extremely nasty billy club and rapping it sharply into the palm of his free hand. Laskin turned his eyes to the ceiling where the fluorescent light was blinking in a kind of cryptic Morse code. Perhaps his guardian angel was signalling him from above. But could he crack the code? At length Laskin said, "While I'm not an IQ specialist, I'd say that your sons, based solely on their appearance in this unflattering light, could very well be idiots. Yes." The atmosphere immediately lightened, the sons became jovial and Mr. Big clapped him on the back. Laskin had cleared the final hurdle.

Status update, 18 January 2013

It was their thirtieth anniversary. Howard noted with satisfaction, as he awoke, that he was half-erect. Bea was in her reliable pretzel twist state beside him (babbling and sweating her way through the last act of one of her zany nightmares). He smiled. They had remained, through all the ups and downs, perfect strangers to one another. "Your thoughts are your business," he'd told her long ago. And he'd meant it.

Status update, 09 June 2011

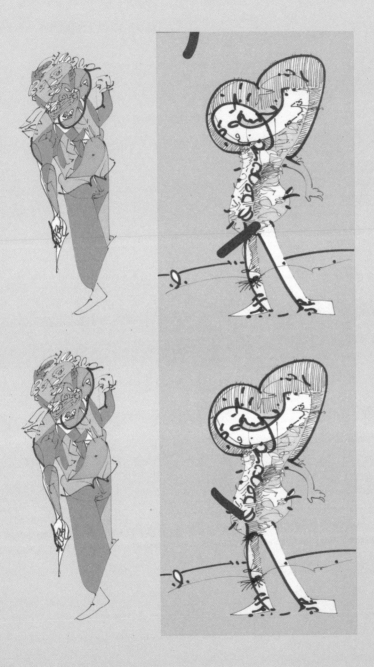

Allen was running a little ahead of schedule today, so he slowed down to give his bullies a chance to catch up. His great fear of them was exceeded only by his love of routine.

Status update, 08 November 2010

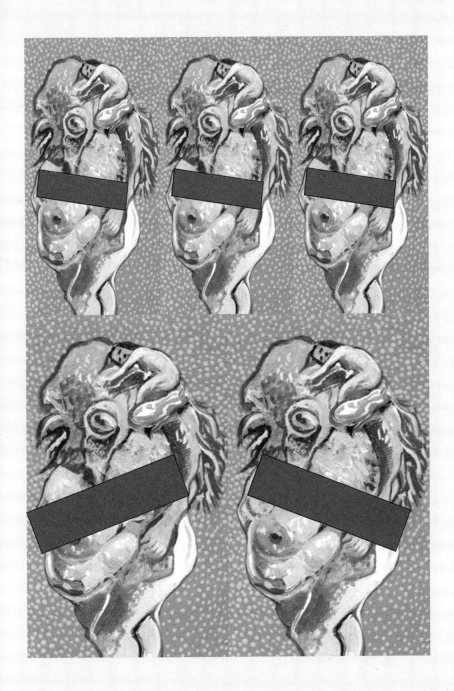

Mme. Pringle skiproped in her garden at dusk, surrounded by bursting buds. She made up skipping rhymes about all the men she had loved and tossed away, with nary a backward glance. Old faithful Clyde, who cleaned her shoes and boots till they shone, watched her from the window, his Adam's apple protruding hugely from his thin neck. He carried her name in his mouth like a trapped bee.

Status update, 14 August 2009

In the liberty-laden, pre-seatbelt days of the 1950s, brand new parents drove their infants home from the hospital in convertibles with big fins. More often than not, they kept the top down to catch the strong breeze, and the babies would blow away to become part of the mounds of freeway litter. There is no bringing back the Easy Come Easy Go spirit of that prosperous era.

Status update, 01 January 2011

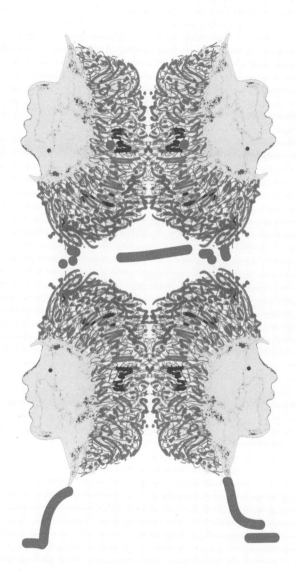

Trent had been clean for eleven months. He marveled at how this snowy day in late spring had yielded such perfect contentment. He was climbing over a fence when he experienced one of those rare, eerie realizations that he was connected to every-thing else that was going on everywhere. His stomach knotted in pained delight. He was certain he would never forget this moment. But after a while, he did.

Status update, 03 May 2011

"When you found me I was just a lost puppy," Sarah told Warthouse Sid, who needed cheering up. "You taught me how to be a mangy cur."

Status update, 27 October 2011

The foremost pleasure of owning a stretch of beach at the lake was, of course, telling intruders that they were trespassing on it, and to send them packing. Myrtle Godwin, 85, was a proud beach mogul, and sat in her chair during the long August afternoons, waiting for passersby to talk to about property lines and the impossibility of making exceptions for one. "Others would soon appear, expecting the same treatment." Myrtle spent a good deal of time listening to the waves. Sometimes she could make out her deceased husband Lester's voice there, telling her of his bridge scores in the afterlife. She wore her fake diamond earrings to feel a little more queenly among the rocks and gulls. Her real diamond earrings were in a safe deposit box, out of harm's way. Truth be told, she was lonely and enjoyed chatting with trespassers, after admonishing them. This afternoon, a lanky young fellow carrying a red book happened by. After asking him why he ignored the signs, she mentioned the book he was carrying, as though it needed to be accounted for. "It's the works of Playdough," she thought he said. She was hard of hearing, and wasn't going to have him repeat himself. She knew nothing of Playdough. She told him she was reading "The Doctor Digs a Grave." He nodded politely. She waited for him to compliment the layout of her beachfront. He said that it must be nice to be so close to the water. She agreed, then listed her favorite features – driftwood, shells, seaweed, the nearby lagoon – with her pet names for things. As he strolled off, she reminded him to let his friends know that this area was off-limits, then smiled to take the edge off it.

Status update, 18 August 2013

It had been a long wait, but the inheritance settlement for the meek finally arrived in the mail. The earth, bruised and battered almost beyond recognition, was now officially theirs. They danced a meek two-step in celebration.

Status update, 24 April 2011

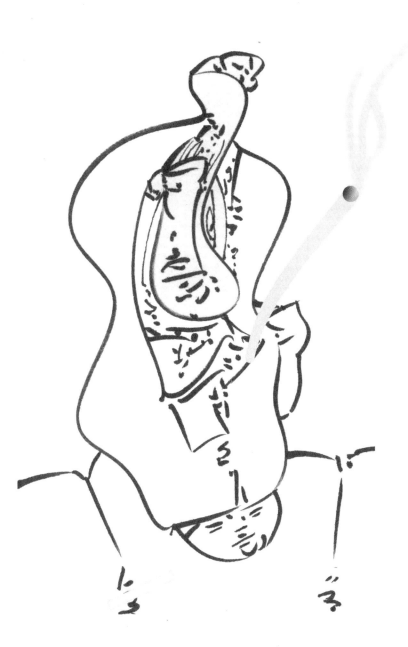

Once Claude accepted the initially irksome word "tightwad" as a self-descrip-tion, the rest was easy. He learned that if he was good enough company, and laughed at his own frugality, he could usually wriggle out of paying his share. "Where's my wallet? Oh no!" Few pleasures equalled stepping ouside for a mouthful of smoke while some cowed acquaintance handed over the plastic.

Status update, 03 February 2010

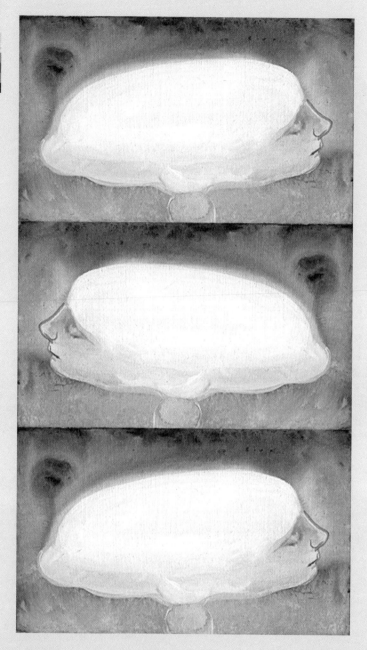

He'd know that laugh of hers anywhere on earth. Its perfect sound had been packed with her bags and taken elsewhere. Herbert walked in the orchard of vanished love and noticed the softly falling colors, the floating ease of demise. The big unnameable thing, full of sky and light, that he'd always tried to put into words while she was still near was actually no bigger than her laugh, and as irretrievable.

Status update, 08 October 2010

Miles was flabbergasted when his long-time, trusted drug dealer threw off his disguise and revealed his mother, swelled up to the full height of her icy authority. "Talk your way out of this one, you little sack of poison." Miles had wrongly assumed that in this one area of his uncertified life, he was not still tied to her apron strings.

Status update, 10 January 2012

Cathleen re-visited a number of the places that she had once lived in her helter-skelter existence,and discovered, as various soul-stirring memories came back to her, that she had been happy (even to the point of exultation) in each of these locales without quite knowing it. At the time they had struck her as the same dreary melody in different keys , a continuation of the pattern of unchallenging jobs, ill-fated relationships, and ambition-flattening circumstances that she had often referred to as "her lot." Was it possible that she had been having one quiet rendezvous with happiness after another but was too embarrassed – or maybe (crazily) ashamed – to acknowledge it? Had she been excessively loyal to the image of herself as someone fated to be unfortunate, the girl left out of every winner's circle? As Cathleen completed her farewell tour of her past "to date", it seemed that there was an amusing, curious, endearingly bright-eyed and enterprising figure trapped in her rigid, false picture of what had happened to her. She caught up at last with Cathleen, age six, laughing about the stories she made up about all the solemn and cheerful animals on her wallpaper.

Status update, 10 April 2012

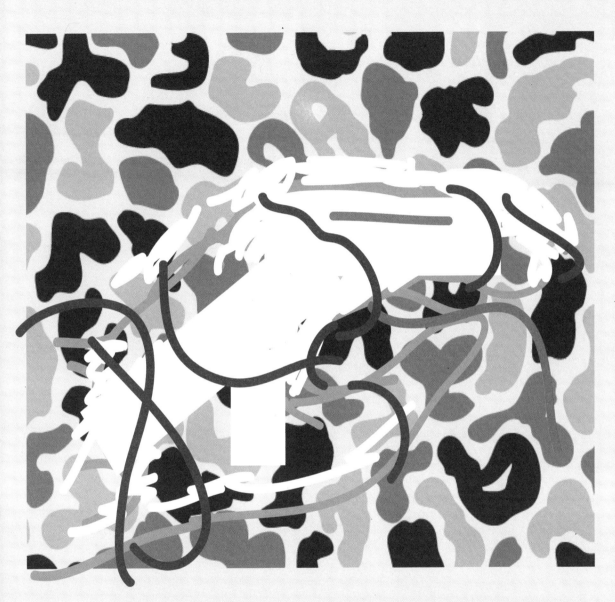

Jeremy watched anxiously as Melanie's thumb and index finger slowly moved toward each other, within half an inch of touching. The words she had last spoken, "This much," in answer to his foolish query, "How much do you still care about me?" echoed in his marshy brain like a snake rattle. He pushed the Kiwi shoelaces he had just purchased into the space remaining so the fingers could not crush him out.

Status update, 15 November 2009

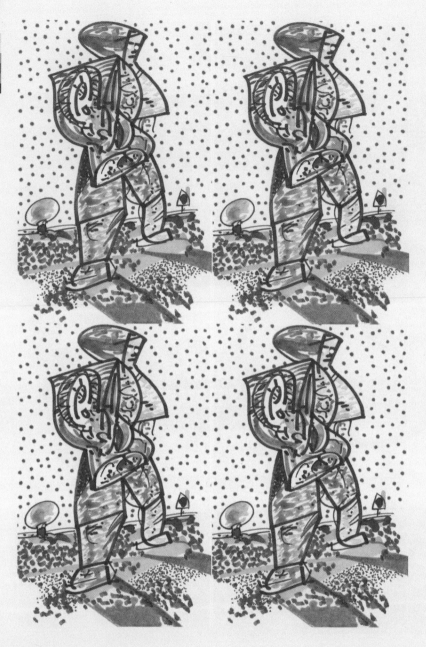

His thoughts were familiar but disquieting, like the road back home from the hospital.

Status update, 26 October 2013

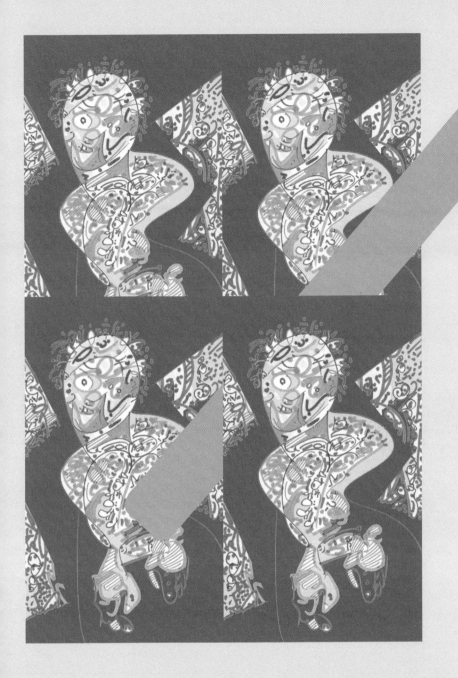

When Albert jokingly asked the dogeared, dogtired hot dog vendor if he could list all the ingredients in his footlonger, he wasn't expecting an answer, and certainly not such a thorough one. Once the sun-baked entrepreneur started rhyming the components around the middle of the list (weasel tits and leper bits) and broke into a little soft shoe routine, Albert found himself inching closer – shudder by shudder – to vegetarianism.

Status update, 03 August 2012

As far as the darkness in my room is concerned, I could be just anybody.

Status update, 12 October 2009

His old downstairs phone always connected him to a switchboard operator named Cora, perhaps the last of her kind. She would speak to him briefly about the jitter-buggers or a new set of twins somewhere or Dudley, the man who cleaned her eavestroughs before punching his call through. Her voice was crisp yet soft, like the guest linen in one of his grandmother's special drawers.

Status update, 14 March 2011

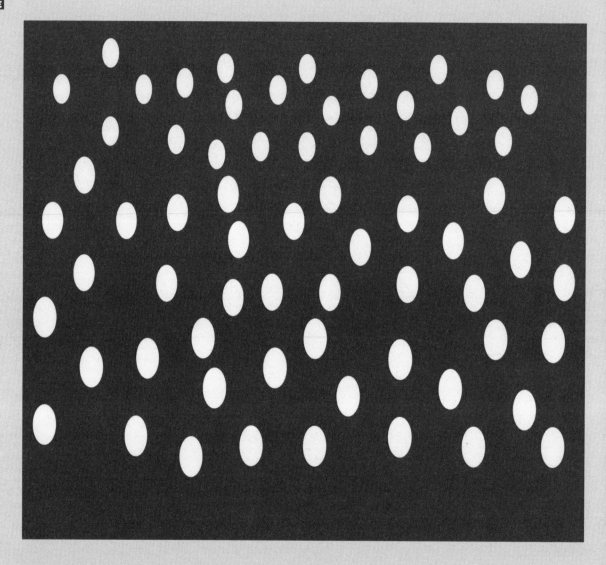

He had said the unforgivable thing. The rational part of him – which was just a sliver of him, really – understood that instantly. There was an unbearable tension and silence encasing her. But another part of him was giddy in the midst of shudders. He felt he was onstage and that he had just delivered a perfectly timed joke. The air was electric. Any second the audience would erupt with laughter and applause.

Status update, 11 January 2011

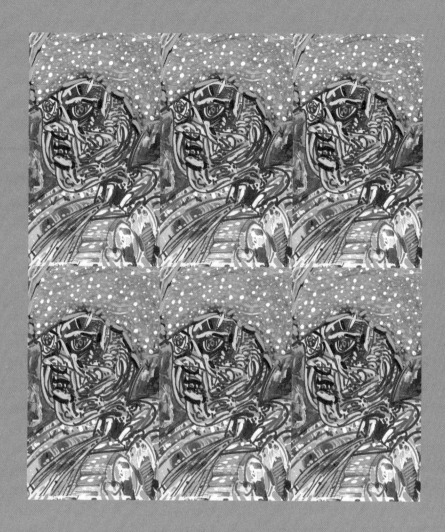

Rex never really apologized to anyone. When push came to shove and it was a matter of keeping his job or getting sex again, he always cleverly said "Sari" instead of "Sorry." And, to make it a double whammy, he made sure to cross his fingers in his pocket or behind his back. It worked like a charm; the remorse-seekers were taken in every time. Another of Rex's pet peeves was scientific evidence. People used it left and right (but mostly left) to sell the hardcore gullible a bill of goods. It didn't take even a lick of common sense to figure out that climate change was a load of horse pucky. "The snow ain't warm, man." But the science crowd's even bigger scam was the notion that human beings were a sack of organs. A lot of doctors – whose one organ that mattered was usually the size of a pencil stub – had gotten rich off that one. Rex would grant that there was flesh and blood and some bones, but that's as far as he would go. He knew he was solid straight through, a badass blockade of meat.

Status update, 13 December 2011

Father was contented when he sat down with his model trains. His two children watched the change that came over him with astonishment and relief. It was like a teabag of bliss being lowered slowly into a dank, shabby mug. He would patiently explain all the improvements he'd made to the station, the little toy town, the general landscape since the last time. He would pick up the new oil car and say, "Have you ever seen such a yellow? It just gleams." He might then shake his head admiringly and say "Boy." On certain evenings, when he hadn't been drinking, he would douse the lights and invite his son and daughter to lie down right next to the track to gain the right perspective. The lights by the station were on and the plastic grazing cows on the hillock were tranquilly in shadow. Father told them that the train's whistle in the night was the world's sweetest, loneliest sound, and as the small, striving engine bore down on them with its own wee headlight searching them out, they believed him.

Status update, 16 August 2012

He turned in his raffle ticket stub to the firing squad officer and claimed his prize.

Status update, 11 October 2013

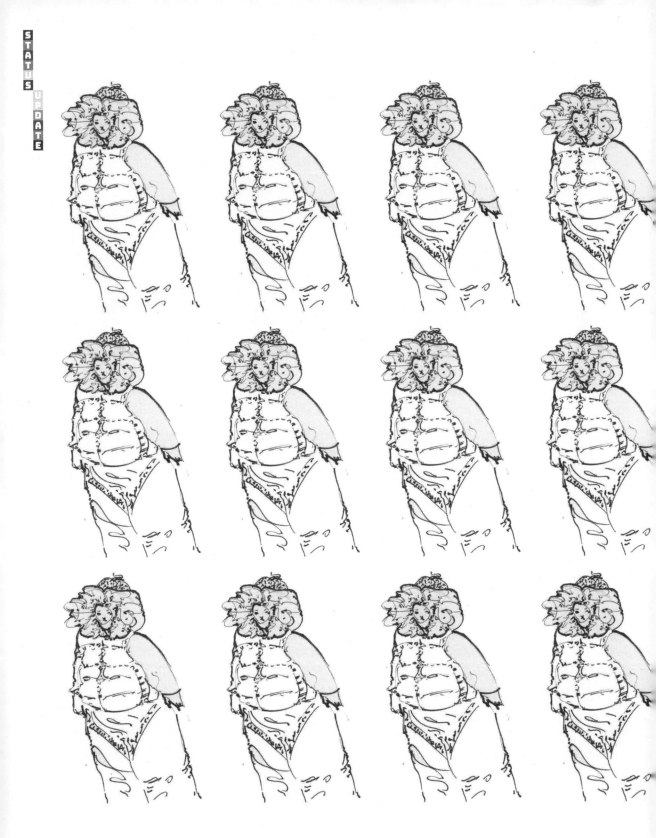

She was so weary of him taking his good moods out on her.

Status update, 13 June 2010

Nora let out a cackle as she climaxed. "What was that all about?" Jason asked, when the laughter subsided. "Don't worry," she said, stroking his cheek. "I wasn't thinking about you."

Status update, 05 January 2013

All it takes is one cold, hard parental slap to turn a child into a statue, a statue that can be revisited year after year in the museum of memory. Renee walked down the familiar museum corridor to the room that she knew best. It contained her mother's Greatest Disappointments, and her small, hawk-eyed likeness was right at the center.

Status update, 29 April 2010

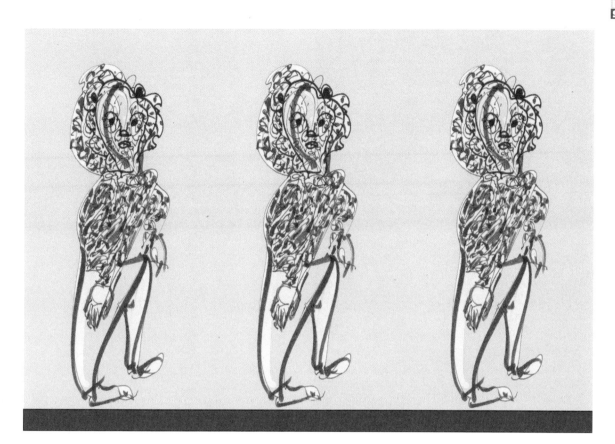

Barb came in, panting breathlessly, and, in her inimitable fashion, called out, "Did I miss it?" The embers in the fireplace, the other guests putting on their coats, the empty glasses, and trailing-off art talk provided an answer. Barb couldn't exactly reconstruct the circumstances that caused her delay; it just seemed that a lot of things had accumulated, and she had trouble getting out from under in time for the gathering, though she was sure she'd been looking forward to it. On her way home, Barb thought about turning fifty, and the embarrassingly large number of things within easy reach that she seemed to have missed out on, without exactly meaning to, or knowing why. It felt to her, in her present discombobulated state, that she just might have missed everything in her life to date, or nearly everything. Was that possible? Missing your life every day, by inches or miles. Well, there was still time. The fog could clear. When the curtain rose on tomorrow, she was determined to be sitting front row center.

Status update, 22 November 2011

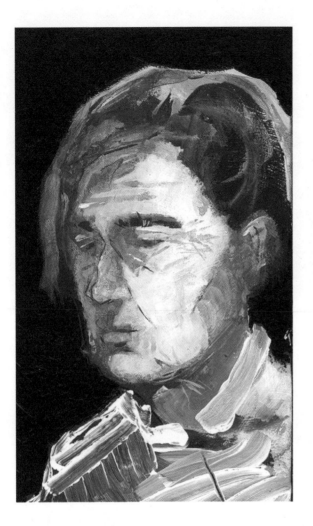

Borden was the prompter at Light and Lively Dinner Theatre. A prompter was necessary because the former sitcom stars that were so often hired for major roles tended to be heavy imbibers who had difficulty recalling their lines, and sometimes which character they were playing. On many nights Borden got to speak the best dialogue in the play, yet though he did so with expression, it was never loud enough to gladden or sadden an audience member's heart. The clanking of silverware, refilling of glasses and steady chewing among the spectators provided thorough cover for him. He was the secret soul of these wispy mysteries and chuckle-strewn romances, hanging on every word and pause, blowing the embers back to life when they threatened to die out. Borden's job was to keep faith no matter what, and he did, crouching on his arthritic haunches in the shadows.

Status update, 18 December 2011

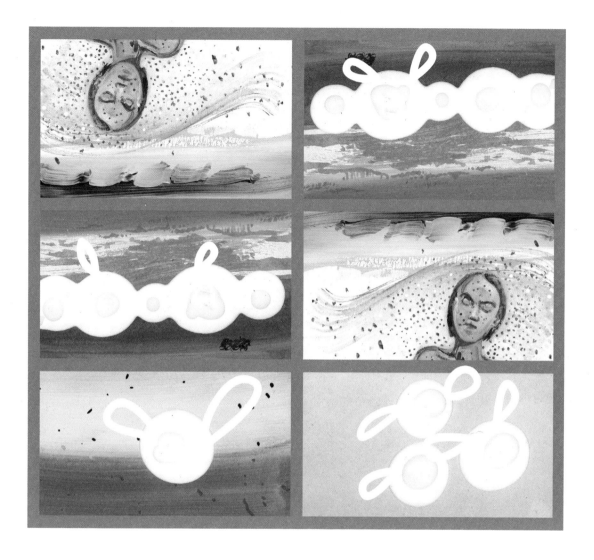

Suzanne has a wonderfully chilly, choosy heart. She burnt her toast this morning, then hurriedly ate three scrambled eggs, sprinkled with tabasco sauce. Her hair is one of her best features, but it hasn't been combed yet. Suzanne's mother would say she looks like an unmade bed. A secret admirer once sent her a note addressing her as the snake lady, telling her she had strange allure. She has a recurring dream about being ashamed for not knowing the right answer. These paltry details are all that will ever be known about Suzanne. She is fated never to appear in another story, even one as small as this. She is lying on the divan now, looking right at you, reader. She bids you a fond farewell.

Status update, 22 July 2013

Ben liked plays where you get to touch the actors you like and then take them home and cover them with wet plaster.

Status update, 17 July 2010

Dave wanted to get to the bottom of this "responsibility' thing. Until recently he'd shared the common view that responsibility was what other people should take more of. But now it seemed it was his turn to take some responsibility. He needed to figure out what exactly he was responsible for. They used to say he was not responsible for his terrible upbringing, for his poverty, for the early death of his mother, for his father's drinking, for the lousy school he went to. He didn't think he was responsible for his heart condition, for the downsizing of the company he worked for, for the loss of his job or the difficulty he was facing getting another one. He had read some articles that told him he wasn't responsible for his children's unhappiness or poor choices, past a certain point, or for the social conditioning he and they were daily subject to. The dismal values of the culture could not be laid, more than a little bit, at his door. Maybe what he was responsible for was not shutting up about his problems enough. Dave decided that he was voluntarily going to assume responsibility for the Second World War. Surely that would be more than his fair share, and he could go back to thinking about other things.

Status update, 16 September 2012

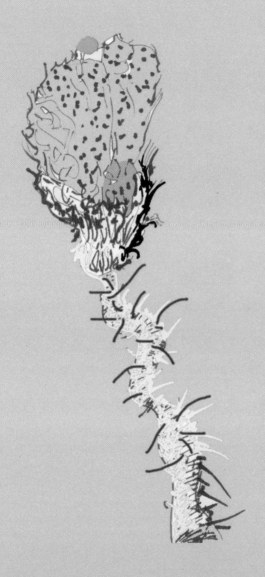

As usual, Mark had failed to make the necessary preparations. And as usual, he was double booked and running late. It started to rain. "I'm so tired of this SHIT," he cried, to no cloud in particular. Mark draped his father's body, clad in his best jogging suit, over a large gravestone. He pinned two crisp twenties to the jacket and a note to the gravedigger. "Whenever you get the chance." As he checked his watch, a last minute inspiration. A sprig of wildflower over dad's ear.

Status update, 19 August 2011

Although Bruce's mother had been dead for six months, his daily phone calls to her had become no less acrimonious. She had added a calm "You put me here" to her long list of grievances, and there was simply no talking (or shouting) her way to reasonableness. "I don't mean to alarm you, Bruce, but the consensus among my new acquaintances is that you're going to wind up in hell. I try to put in a good word, of course, but they're no fools. They know I'm neglected, and how little you did for me when it might have made all the difference." Bruce couldn't stop pleading his case, but he detected a new coldness and distance in her manner. He felt like crying, but tears had never made an impression on her. She would only laugh and call him Liberace.

Status update, 04 February 2012

The boy was too poor to get a ticket for the carousel, yet lingered nearby for hours, watching the other children spinning about on their painted animals in a flurry of music and glitter. He could only accompany them in his imagination. It so happened that the ride he yearned for and imagined himself having was far more extravagant and exhilarating than any literal ride could have been. Unfortunately, he did not know this, nor would he have believed anyone who told him it was so. And he still went to bed hungry that night.

Status update, 04 November 2012

Norma was fond of saying, "Let me look at you." Sometimes she was trying to catch me in a lie but more often her examination led her to spot something good in my face that was less visible to others. She regularly pulled what she called "small treats" for my brother and me out of one of her mysterious, misshapen, dark purses, but they never felt small, because her emotional timing of treats was unerring. Norma told us on many occasions about Steve Linzler, her first and (it was hard not to suspect) only real love. "I asked him to wait for me a few more months. If he had, we would have been together. But he just couldn't wait. He was an impatient man." This Linzler was a china salesman, we learned, and that fact made him sound fragile, as well as impatient. "So, he chose someone else, but spent his too short life regretting his haste, I think, waiting for a second chance that was not to be." I liked thinking about Steve Linzler and Norma hand in hand, trying to run back the way they came, in the fading light, to the beginning of their love. But love was running too, and it was too fast for them. They couldn't catch up. The gate, when they arrived, was shut tight, and the leaves were still.

Status update, 03 December 2011

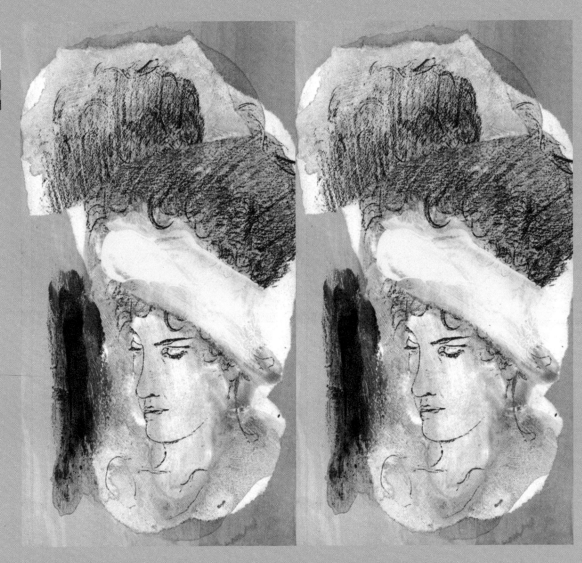

Lorraine was letting her maid, Anita, go because she did not give her the proper respect. Being an honest person, she told Anita that this was the reason for her dismissal, rather than simply leaving her in the dark. She said her work was otherwise satisfactory. "Why do I have to respect you?" Anita asked. "Why is that part of the job? Did you want me to pretend?" Lorraine paused. There was a simple answer to these questions, and Lorraine considered abandoning her usual tact and giving it to her straight. "I am far richer than you and therefore I am better than you." But Anita was not one to waste her clearheadedness on someone who was sure to take even the plainest of truths the wrong way.

Status update, 07 May 2012

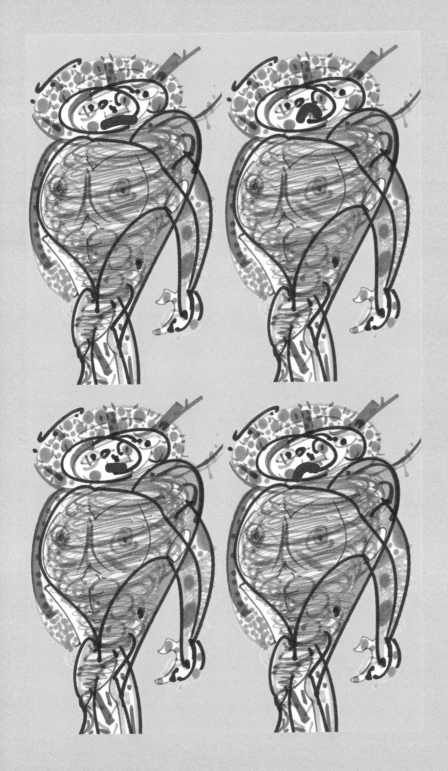

God broke a centuries-long silence to announce that He hadn't yet forgiven anybody for anything.

Status update, 28 April 2012

Beryl had never enjoyed any embraces quite so much as those she practiced by herself in her garage as a young girl. She loved the way she had hugged herself close until her breath quickened, and her perfectly timed pats on the back. Those hands needed no words to offer solace, knew just when to squeeze and release, and had exquisite patience for her slow motion surrenders. Real partners were alarmingly bulky, cumbersome. And frankly their otherness interfered with her giddy delight in her own sense of self. She guessed she was just one of those women who would never get over the raptures of first love.

Status update, 14 March 2012

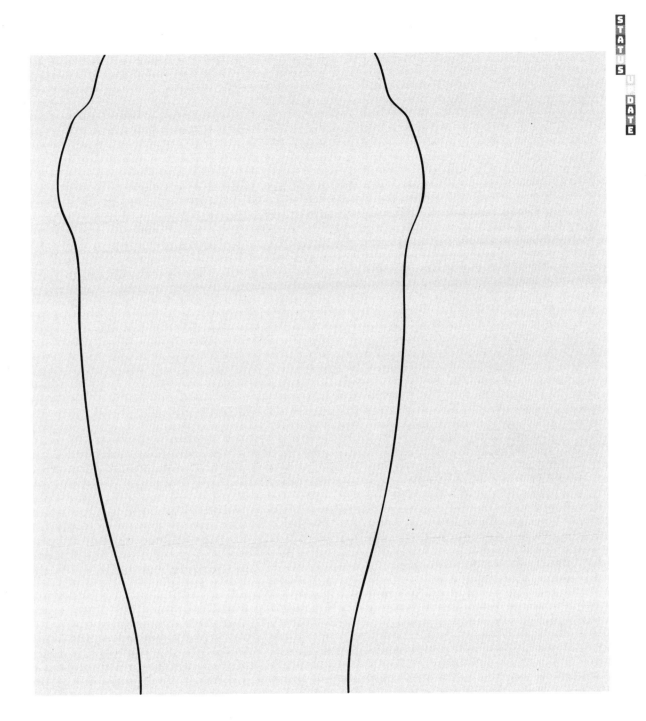

Bruce had never been able to take a compliment. Perhaps it was because his mother in her wisdom had never given him one. He found it deeply unsettling then to feel his stomach and throat tighten and two tears winching their way onto his eyelids when he was praised for his tree drawings by his prison art instructor.

Status update, 13 October 2009

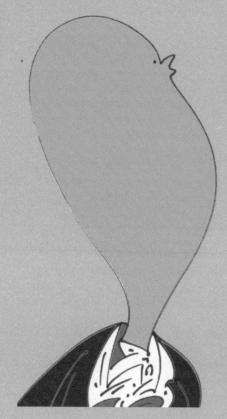

Harris had never doubted that Becky had much greater knowledge and life experience than he did. But this perceived superiority threatened him. He spent most of the time they had together (years, in fact) attempting to catch up and prove that his own inner resources were entirely sufficient to make him an independent, well-fortified person. He did not need to seek her advice on consequential matters, or show his weakness by taking advantage of what she might have to offer him, especially where emotional insight was concerned. Then suddenly, Becky was gone. And in her absence he had no difficulty coming up with a thousand questions he should have have put to her. How he yearned to hear her voice, with its ripple of mischief, answering them, one by one, as she played with the sugar bowl lid, meeting his eyes and then looking down . Why had he expended so much time and energy in protecting himself from knowing her?

Status update, 16 January 2013

Joan's scornful laughter had stopped being the best medicine. He decided that she was kind in all the small ways so that she could stay mean in the really big ones.

Status update, 12 July 2010

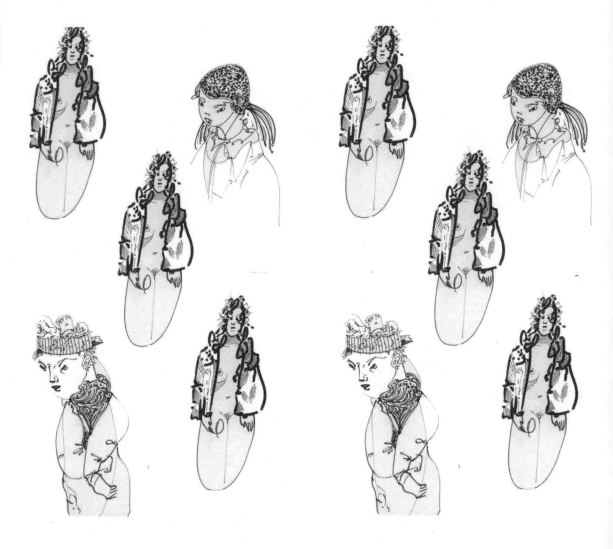

She rose up in her sheer nightgown in revolt against her boyfriend's children, and pursued them through the hallway and down the stairs. They trembled with a strange trembling because they could tell she meant to bring harm, but her beauty excited them deeply in the midst of their fear. At length she locked them in the bathroom with her and told them frightful stories of what would become of them, dipping them in the honey of her madness. They believed her and her mirrored image as she told them her father would take her word against theirs, and they vowed to do exactly as she said from now on, or else. They could not help stealing glances at her fiery red toe polish, and wondered where her thighs ended.

Status update, 10 June 2013

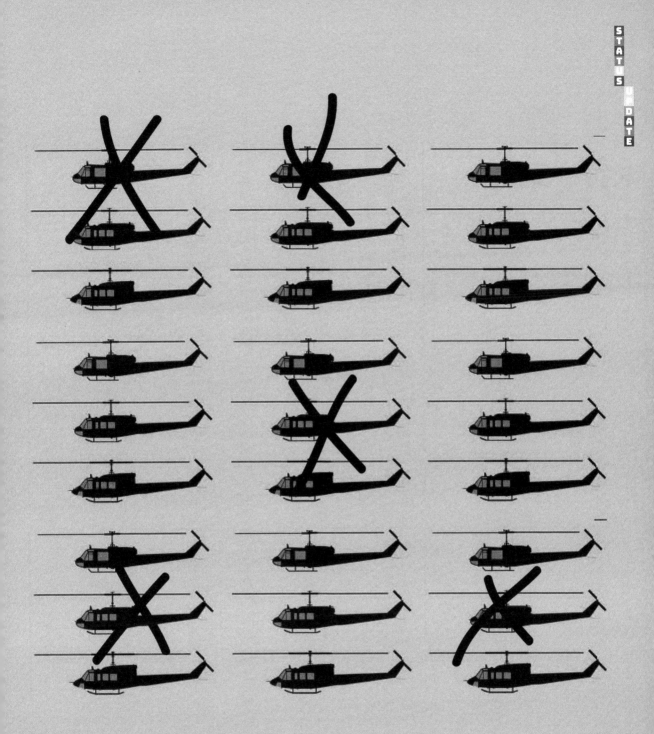

What Vic remembered, with a dull shame, was a sentence from a letter he'd written to his cousin, Paul, from Vietnam: "You'd be amazed how easy it is to kill these little guys."

Status update, 12 November 2011

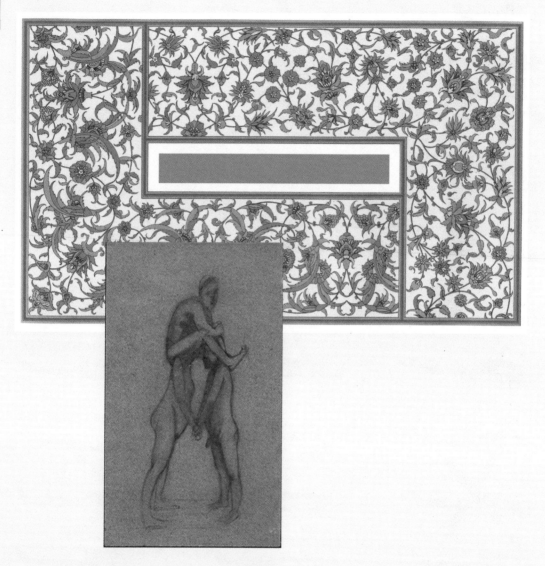

Francis told his son, Adam, that he was proud of him. There was a silence leading up to his brief words, and his voice was soft and gruff. Clearly this was difficult for him. He turned away abruptly after touching Adam on the shoulder and went into the kitchen, Adam sat down, almost shuddering. He had waited for years--maybe his whole life – for this acknowledgement. Then, from the kitchen, came a louder follow-up: "April Fools, Adam."

Status update, 01 April 2012

Whenever anyone told her an engaging anecdote, she assumed it must be a lie. It was next to impossible for her to believe that interesting things really happened to people.

Status update, 13 January 2011

Joan hadn't heard anyone use the word obedience in quite some time. Even God seemed to have grown weary of it. Joan suspected that it would be hard to love those who had learned too well how to bow to commands. Perhaps one could tolerate the perfectly submissive. But the amiable backsliders, and those who chafe against the lessons assigned to them have a chance of seizing their freedom, and making something of it. It's the spectacle of the untamed spirit that brings a welcome riot to the heart.

Status update, 24 January 2012

The sparrow vacated their branch, giving them a bit more room. "Everything tastes better on an up-in-a-tree picnic," said Captain Davy, as he salted his celery stalk. Janet smiled in agreement, and brushed the snow from her lashes.

Status update, 10 February 2010

Hugh thought he recognized the nurse who was tending to him, but he was too weak to crane his head or speak to her. Then, in his growing dizziness, he experienced a wild flash. She was Mae Oslo, a girl who – decades ago – had a crush on him in high school. Her feelings for him were drastically one-sided. It was embarrassing to recall how often he had made fun of her, with the cheerful brutality of the much sought after. "Maypole" was one of the choice nicknames for her he came up with to elicit laughs from his friends. She probably didn't remember him at all, physical wreck that he now was. But he was mistaken. A current was still flowing, from this woman who now had his life more or less in her hands. Just before he slipped into a coma he felt her hot breath in his ear, as she hissed: "You will never hold me in your arms."

Status update, 28 January 2013

Brett found it unfair that his random acts of brutality were always in the newspaper,
but his random acts of kindness were generally ignored.

Status update, 18 April 2010

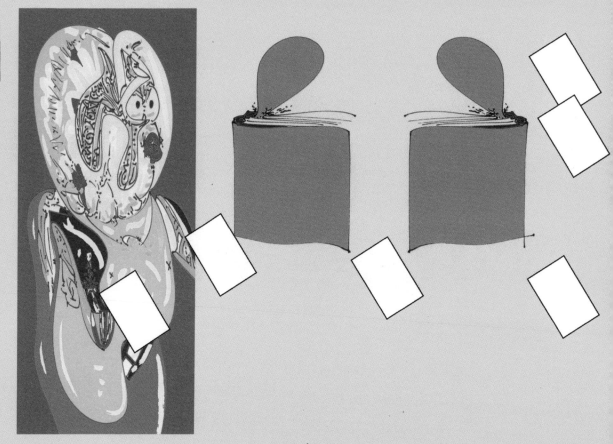

Norris had created a great many files over the years, filled with clippings and his own makeshift reflections on a wide variety of subjects. He had taken considerable care to organize the files meticulously, for the sake of a friendly prospective reader (the Gentle Reader he'd always believed in, and to whom everything was addressed). That reader had never materialized – no doubt being much sought after by a deserving horde of other writers. It now seemed a distinct possibility that Norris's bulky productions were written for no one's eyes but his own. But that thought didn't sadden him. The writing had sustained him while he did it. It had given purpose and shape to his days. The pages made a bright vista, stretching all the way back to youth. He became enamored of the idea of leaving the world as he found it. He was a privileged wayfarer who passed through the country of his life gratefully, not wishing or needing to leave traces. The approaching end was a time for tranquil shedding. Vanity at this juncture was just extra weight.

Status update, 04 January 2012

It usually took him the first half of the day to figure out what he really wanted to do, and the rest of the day to discover why he couldn't possibly get around to it just yet.

Status update, 01 July 2009

He touched the purple Easter egg of her eye, so immense now and swollen shut. This slow-moving finger of his, by the time it reached her hair, had attained an oddly soothing power. It felt tender and anxious, having broken its ties with the fist that had done the damage.

Status update, 23 October 2010

Wherever innocent bystanders chose to gather, Oswald could be found among them, gazing at the designated accident or spectacle with exactly the right level of concern, hope, or trepidation. He didn't care to brag, but he was, in truth, the most innocent bystander of them all.

Status update, 06 February 2012

"Could there ever be another day as happy as this one?" she wondered. As she looked up at the drapery of starlight, it struck her afresh that the light burning above was in fact the light of the past, making its way toward her over immeasurable temporal distances. Although some of the stars – who could say which? – were no more, they were bearing light still, offering themselves to her gaze as beauty and thoughtless comfort. She felt the happiness that had descended on her with such power for a handful of hours was there in the starlight. It was and is, and was would keep it so.

Status update, 03 October 2013

Whenever George needed a self-esteem boost, he wandered over to the Prospect Lawn Cemetery, jumped on a few graves and exclaimed, "Ha ha, you're DEAD and I'm not!"

Status update, 06 July 2009

Linda had claimed to love Cyrus's way of disengaging himself from the crazed workaday whirl. Cyrus would sit on his haunches dreamily and make the world a friendlier, sweeter place, like Ferdinand the Bull. Let others push and shove their way to fictions of higher status. He renounced competition and the unsightly spasms of careerists comparing resumes. But one day Linda re-wrote the relationship contract. She laid into Cyrus with all her might, deriding as useless what formerly seemed his lovely virtues. "Your real problem is that you don't care enough about anything to try. Your passivity masks a deep-seated fear of failure. You don't have any guts and you somehow arrange things so that this lack of courage and goals appears to you and others as moral superiority." Cyrus was uncertain if she said these hurtful things out of concerned love for him or because she had lost her love and none of it any longer made a difference. He decided not to defend himself. He sat in his chair looking at her. How beautiful a person she was, even in her rage. Cyrus felt like a pear tree weighed down with ripe fruit that would not, could not fall.

Status update, 06 September 2012

Beverly went to the big Schuster family reunion, against her better judgment. The first twenty people she spoke with commended her on how tall she was. Though she wished they had maintained a discreet silence on this sore point, it was better than being praised as Junoesque or Amazonian by her sharp-witted friends. Late in the afternoon after being shown a napping, ill-looking iguana by its mean-looking child owner and telling him for some reason that "he must be proud to have one," she found herself stranded at a picnic table with a desolate man named Herman, who was apparently a third cousin. Herman had a shoebox filled with photos that he shared with her. He began with some candids that a detective had taken of his wife, Ernestine, in bed with another man. "Quite a shock," he opined. Further down there were photos of his son, Zeeter, strapped in an electric chair in Oklahoma. "I can't say that he didn't deserve it. Zeeter was a rotten apple. His head didn't catch on fire as some do, and that was a mercy." Beverly tried to find more reassuring images and picked up one of an apple tree. But, as she looked closer, there was a child falling out of it. Herman was still talking. "You've got to take the bad with the good, I always say. And you sometimes wonder why things happen the way they do. But people rely too much on explanations these days."

Status update, 11 September 2012

She said he could change but only if he really wanted to. He took her words to heart, and over time managed to change for the worse.

Status update, 13 February 2010

It was one of those North Pole moods again. He knew that a man's gotta do what a man's gotta do, but he had difficulty explaining to himself why this was so. At such times, the often blurry figure of Irma Claus came into focus for him. "You still believe in me, don't you?" he asked, trying not to sound too beseeching. She gave him his freshly laundered sack, and replied carefully. "Your fame, like that of many people, is based on a misunderstanding. And at the beginning, the misunderstanding had to do with something beautiful." She became silent. If more reassurance was necessary, he would have to talk with the reindeer.

Status update, 25 December 2011

Marcia's seventeen year old son, Burt, had been missing for three days. She had trouble summoning the feelings she knew she was supposed to have: panic, heart-ache, the feverish resolve to participate in a massive search. The trouble was, he had left at such short notice. His timing, as so often, was off. Marcia was not an emotional multi-tasker. She was still in the midst of mourning for her cat, Periwinkle. As she passed Burt's room she thought again of calling the police, in case he really meant business, and wasn't going to turn up and embarrass her. She thought hurriedly that his room might look better if it was painted avocado green.

Status update, 20 October 2012

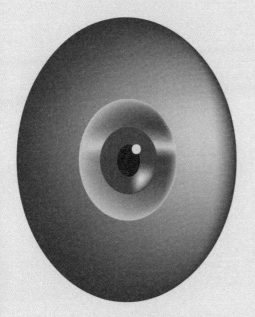 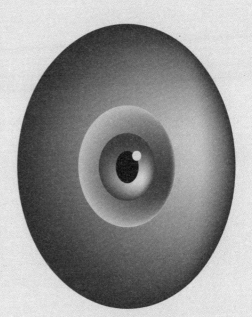

There was a sea of loving kindness in her eyes, but he had never learned to swim.

Status update, 18 March 2010

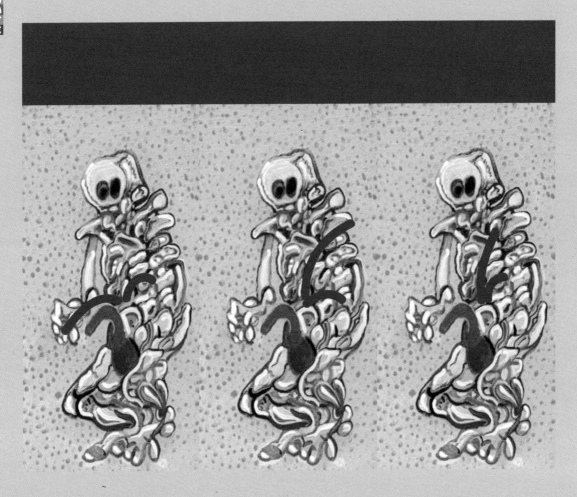

Ruth always tried to be attentive to the needs of her guests. Others might ignore the skeleton who was always showing up at her feasts, but she tried to make him feel welcome. Though the skeleton (she thought of him as Sheldon) was not a mingler, she set up a xylophone for him in the corner in case he felt like jamming a bit. "Beautiful Dreamer" was a song he liked; she wished he would occasionally play something else. Ruth regularly set a place for him at the table. He had little use for food, but the thrush who had taken up residence in his rib cage (a pet?) would gratefully peck at the sprouts and cranberries. Ruth was drawn to Sheldon's lonely ways, but she had heard from reliable sources that he had a mean streak.

Status update, 06 January 2012

Who would ever have guessed that such mundane, unpromising shit would one day hit the fan?

Status update, 17 July 2013

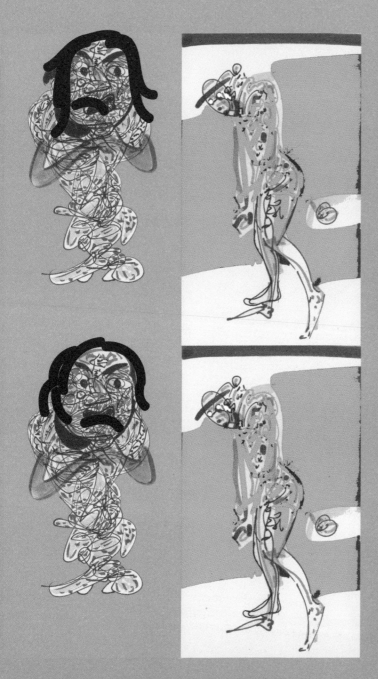

She vowed that her hated for him would never wither away. It would easily outlast his own life, and would prove stronger by far than her love had ever been. She would keep faith with it until she had drawn her last breath, and pass it on to her children so they could burn with it in her absence. She finally had his full attention. He was not only moved, but reassured.

Status update, 02 September 2010

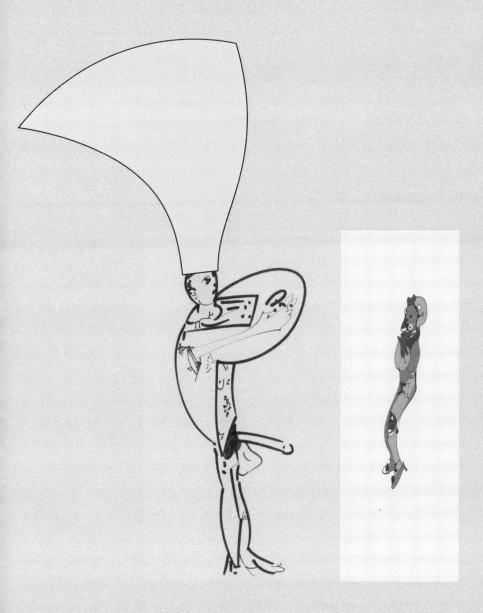

Paolo Gabriele, the Pope's ousted butler, would miss helping the Holy See get dressed and undressed, pouring his tea, and holding the umbrella over him on rainy days. He had been especially pleased and flattered when the Supreme Pontiff would ask him whether he ought to wear this or that robe or crucifix. And in spite of Paolo's concern about the corruption of certain cardinals, his faith remained rock solid. "There is enough Catholic majesty in the Vatican and Rome to shrivel the dick of any Protestant or heathen," he politely told reporters.

Status update, 29 May 2012

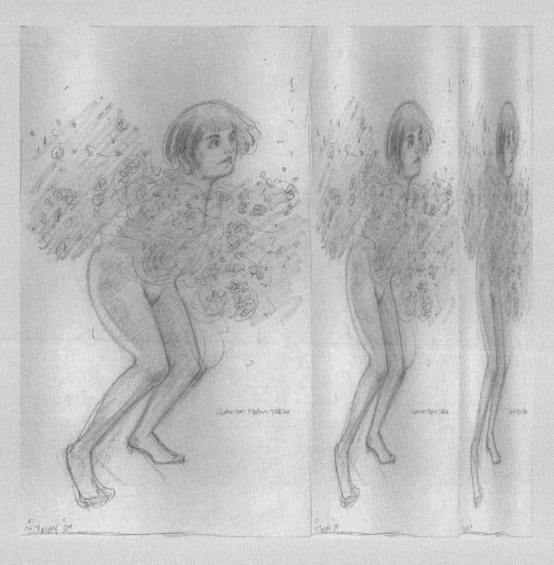

When Beth woke up, she was sitting on the porch steps, waiting. Beside her was a basket of freshly picked beans and a small black suitcase. She opened the suitcase and found a graduation cap, some bottles of India ink, and a charm bracelet. Dorothy Nagel, her best friend in high school, ran up the driveway, more excited than ever. She was waving and telling her to hurry. It had been such a long time since they'd seen one another. Dorothy had died so young. Beth had a pang of worry that she wasn't dressed properly. She was still in her flannel nightgown and barefoot. "Don't be silly," Dorothy said, touching Beth's nose in just the way she used to. "It's come as you are." Beth knew she'd forgotten something important, but this wasn't the time for fretting; it didn't matter. She was ready to go.

Status update, 25 June 2012

She exhausted her resources of inventiveness, as well as her large capacity for taking delight, trying to make him happy in their life together. She came to the conclusion that nothing and no one could make him happy. That truth, while it lasted, gave her considerable consolation. Eventually she gave up on him – anyone would have, long ago, her friends assured her – and they went their separate ways. Soon after, he met Rebecca, with whom he instantly found contentment of a different kind, deeper than anything she had witnessed. He seemed effortlessly, extravagantly in love. How it frustrated her that there was a secret she had never found for securing balance and pleasure, and a romance plot someone else could place him in where things worked out. She made her own good enough choice later on, but part of her was held hostage by this maddening image of him being cured of the unhappiness that she now symbolized.

Status update, 31 August 2013

In the long run it is impossible to conceal completely the sort of person one is, except from oneself.

Status update, 16 February 2010

Hal was driving on the fast moving expressway with his wife and two small children when his engine failed without warning. He was stricken with terror that he had brought them to a senseless end right here, and promised the powers in which he had no belief that he would give anything to make it over to the side of the highway without being demolished. Somehow catastrophe was averted by inches, though blaring horns and swerving vehicles spread their mad colors everywhere. Had it been goodbye, Sharon had not found time to look at him. Her mind was elsewhere. The dust was settling. Before she or the children could say anything, Hal got out of the car and watched himself running frantically toward a grove of oak trees in the far distance. He had promised too much, and he was still stuck in the thought that all was lost. When he arrived at the trees, he saw a brook behind a mass of reeds. This must have been his destination all along. He lay down and pushed his head into the water, holding it under until his breath gave out. He was a free man, an old movie voice kept whispering inside him. He was on the edge of every possible thing. Hal rested in the grace of the world, cleansed for the moment of fear and foreknowledge. Then he stood up and turned back, waiting for the life that was his to catch up with him.

Status update, 19 September 2012

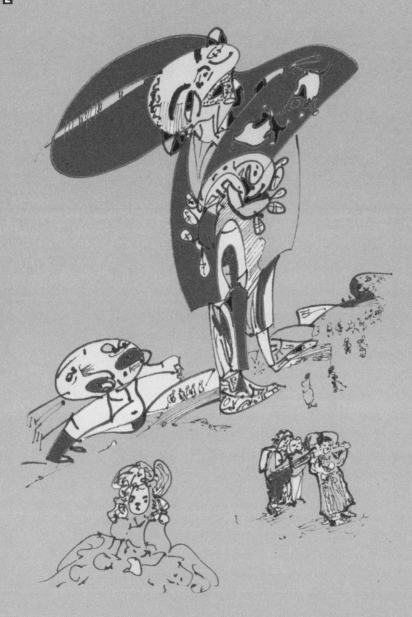

Howard painstakingly described himself to Linda, who was beginning to get the picture. He had many views and interests, and there were many different parts to his character and his 'complicated' life history, but the glue that held it all together was dullness.

Status update, 28 May 2012

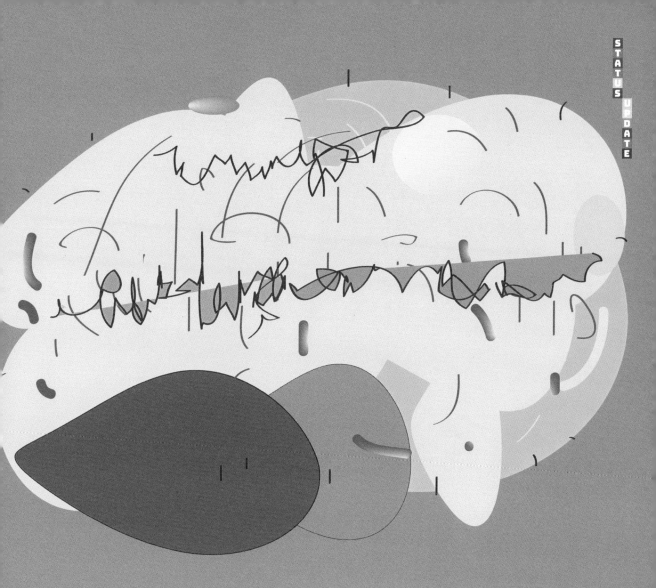

Having to peel 2000 potatoes on an overcast Saturday gave Andre time to think about his future. He wanted to be famous in a hurry so he would still have the excuse of being young and unbridled for treating his groupies badly. In order to achieve fame according to this timetable, he would have to learn how to stand up to himself, and to oppose every day his natural inclination to make as little effort as possible. Once sweet renown was within his grasp, he would have plenty of time to become disillusioned with it, and slowly indulge in the various vices that eased the pain. Then Andre, by the time he was forty, would willingly retire from the fray and go back to contented obscurity. He could see himself, on a Saturday far in the future, peeling potatoes with a humble heart and enjoying it.

Status update, 18 February 2012

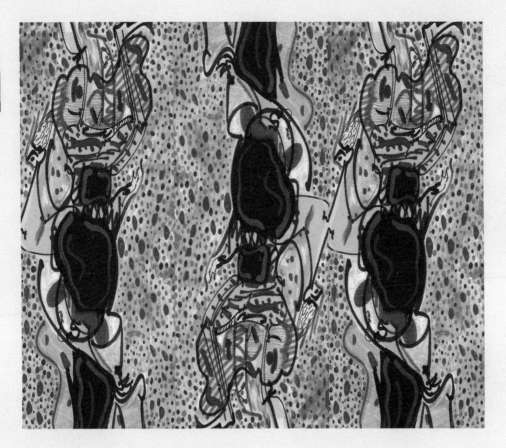

Marie was bowled over by how good Death was in bed. When she thought it over, she decided it shouldn't have been that much of a surprise. Death had spent plenty of time in bedrooms over the milennia, and, being as observant as he was, learned a great deal about what women like and don't like. Marie had not been nearly as ill as Death had expected, so he changed his plans and – with her consent – settled in for an afternoon of "on the edge" romancing. His feet were cold at first, but he was most solicitous about her fears and completely understandable trust issues, and was willing to take it slow. (Even though he had other appointments, he whispered "They'll just have to wait," which made Marie feel special.) He told her that if she wanted to know the supreme rapture of love, she needed to really let go, but there seemed to be a slippery dark slope in view that made her hold back a little. Death was patient, and smiled as he brushed back her hair. "There's always next time." Death left his cloak behind, assuring her that he took their new relationship seriously, and was not afraid of commitment. She held his cloak up to her nose and inhaled deeply; it smelled of rain and strawberries.

Status update, 13 April 2012

His father always had a special knack of being more present when he was away.

Status update, 20 June 2010

He asked Maureen to bend close so she could hear him. He admitted in a hoarse whisper to all his wrongdoing, repented of it, and said he hoped (though he was utterly unworthy) that she might some day find it in her heart to forgive him. He wanted to make things right at last. Maureen began to shake him violently, screaming, "Take it back. Take it back. You are not, not, not going to die in peace or go to heaven."

Status update, 03 July 2012

Last night remained so real to him. He thought if he merely reached his arm behind him, without looking, he might still touch its giddy, impassioned radiance. He felt as he did as a boy one long ago Christmas morning, when he was grandly alone, creeping about with no one's permission in his home before dawn, savoring the darkness, venturing near the tree but not breaking the spell by letting his eyes rest on what was waiting there.

Status update, 04 December 2013

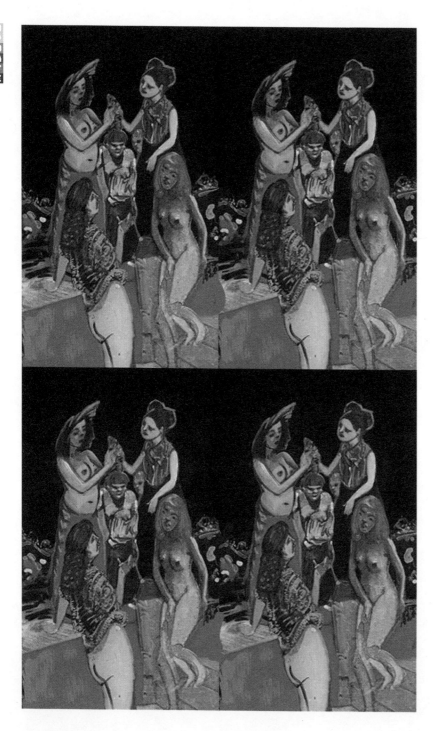

All they needed to become a real family again was for the neighbors to have another great tragedy.

Status update, 22 June 2010

Annie could not imagine why so many people disliked getting advice from others. There was nothing she enjoyed more than seeking counsel when in doubt or difficulty. Her blue-eyed gaze would be transfixed as someone, just about anyone, took the trouble to lay out out the alternatives for her or offered guidance based on past experience. She nodded vigorously as she drank it all in. But Annie was incapable of following or even remembering any of the suggestions presented to her. The words might as well have been delivered in a foreign language. It was the pleasing sound of attentive concern that kept Annie so innocently enthralled. And tomorrow she would be back for more – a perfectly clean slate, eager to start at the very beginning and to have everything re-explained as she basked in the glow of the speaker's fascinating, useless authority.

Status update, 01 August 2013

He became convinced as an eight year old that if his parents went for a short trip or even out for an evening that they would never return home unless he spent a certain number of hours sitting in the war chair in the attic. (The name "war chair" was somewhat obscure. The chair had occupied its present spot for a very long time, perhaps since "the war" was still on.) He had converted his fears and sense of powerlessness into a demanding task that he alone could perform. It felt necessary for some reason that he not turn the light on and that he sit very still in his assigned seat. He could often hear the rustle of small animals inside the walls. As his eyes adjusted to the darkness, he peered through it at what he knew were the forms of old trunks and hanging garments and an ancient sewing machine. He smelled the combined smells of yesteryear as he waited there, concentrating on steering his endangered, forgetful parents to safety. They would overcome the mounting threats and make their way back. He once told his grandmother, who had searched high and low for him, what he was up to. She sat on the attic floor for a spell, right beside him, and then informed him that the rocking chair in her room was used for the very same purpose as the war chair. It had even more power, as a matter of fact, and she would be happy if he would now and then relieve her at her post. They would work together to make sure that everything was all right. "I was trained as a night watch-man, you see. I'm very good at it." So many years later, after she and his mother and father were gone for good, he still rocked now and then in grandmother's chair. Tonight he remembered her hand on his arm in the attic darkness and her firm voice, which never made light of his worries. Though he had lost all his power to protect what he loved, the rocker's pulse still held her somehow, and helped him push his way through the troubles of this late hour.

Status update, 16 November 2012

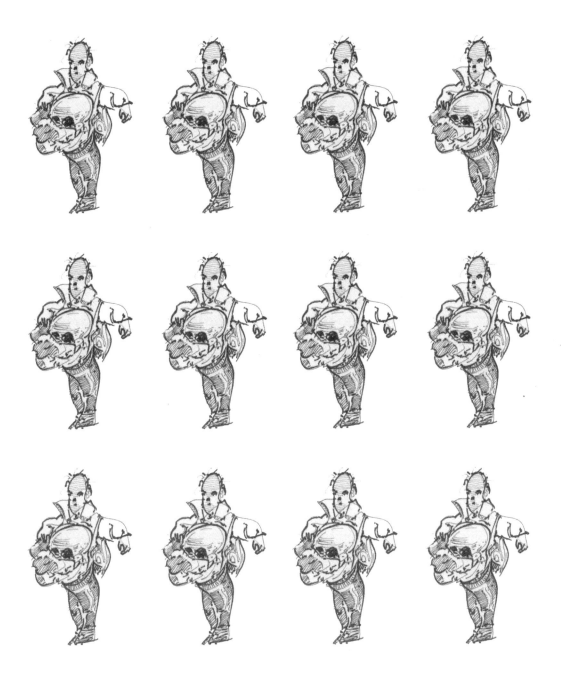

Rather late in life, Martin summoned the courage to confront his many fears, and laid them to rest, one by one. Not long after he discovered that they were all that had protected him from a killing boredom. It was fear, and fear alone, that had made his life seem so full.

Status update, 08 May 2011

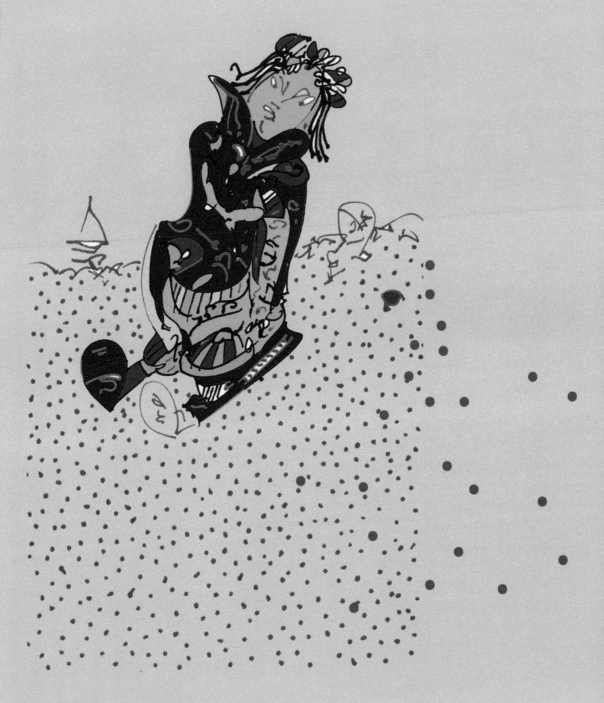

Maisie was trying to determine if it was her heart, or her vagina, that was broken.

Status update, 28 July 2012

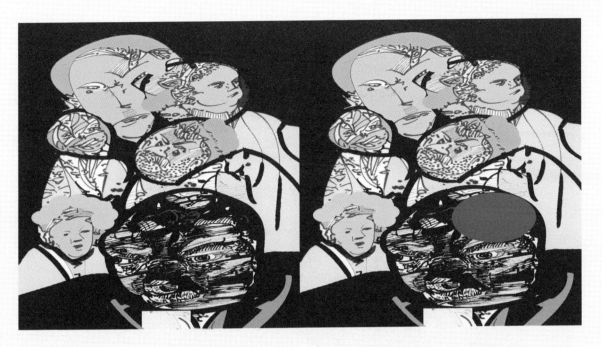

Brady stopped over at our house as a luncheon guest one blustery afternoon. He may have been invited by mistake, as far as mother could later figure out. The luncheon was over in two hours, but after many years Brady was still in our midst, acquiring more and more bulk and lethargy as he clumped about in a tedious parody of locomotion, or sat like a giant prow sculpture at our kitchen table. Our young imaginations, once supple and lively, were ground to dust attempting to understand why mother never got him to leave. Her otherwise strong will seemed to evaporate when confronted with Brady's stubbornly rooted presence, his terrifying need to place himself forever in her care, as a creature beyond control, an eater without limits. We wondered if mother had been permanently hypnotized to bring him heaping platefuls of casserole and stew, which Brady would linger over for what seemed hours of audible chewing, swallowing, and slurping. His conversation was mercifully confined to the sounds he emitted, capped at the end by a thunderous sigh of satisfaction and a smiling stomach pat. Now and again he presented mother with a long cheerio necklace as a token of his gratitude. How we dreaded the inevitable Brady question as he made his way to table in the morning, a cloth napkin already tucked in beneath the folds of his neck. "Are we dining in tonight?"

Status update, 08 December 2012

"I cannot bear your mother's cackling any longer." Stefan was surprised by his father's remark, because he rarely confided in him, and almost never expressed an emotion. Dad wasn't quite through. "Go downstairs and tell your mother I want a divorce."

Status update, 23 July 2009

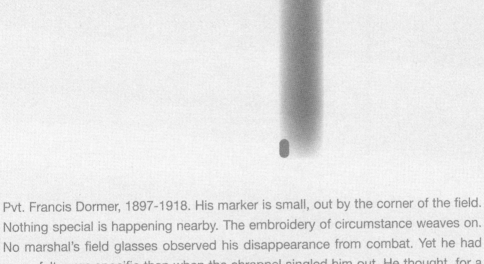

Pvt. Francis Dormer, 1897-1918. His marker is small, out by the corner of the field.
Nothing special is happening nearby. The embroidery of circumstance weaves on.
No marshal's field glasses observed his disappearance from combat. Yet he had
never felt more specific than when the shrapnel singled him out. He thought, for a
few seconds, he had let his loved ones down, going out so young and so far away.

Status update, 12 November 2010

When obliged to attend a party, Sarah found ways to be given a wide berth. Sometimes she introduced herself as an uninvited guest, and warned the person she was talking to not to tell anyone because it was just a little revenge plot she had going. Other times she said she was the cockroach's wife, and pointed at some mild looking gentleman. "He likes to chew the skin off the soles of my feet. Want to see?"

Status update, 17 September 2010

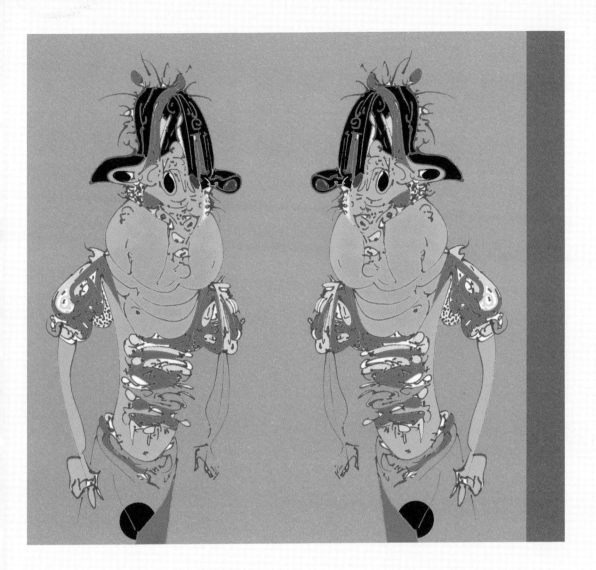

Madame Handke often gave Whitman, her castrated chauffeur, little gifts, to let him know that, barring that sad little twist of fate, he would assuredly have been her one true love. She considerately wore a veil now whenever he drove her anywhere. Since his "loss," he explained, he found Madame's steady, mournful gaze, even in the rearview mirror, too piercing for bodily comfort. The first time she beheld Whitman, in the days of his strength, he stood like a planet of phosphorescent love by the old Steam Mill. His colossal steed snorted impatiently behind him as he whacked the moist cattails by the stream with his riding crop. A thousand frogs croaked melodiously and the water sparkled like shattered glass, as a single bell tolled deep inside her.

Status update, 26 February 2013

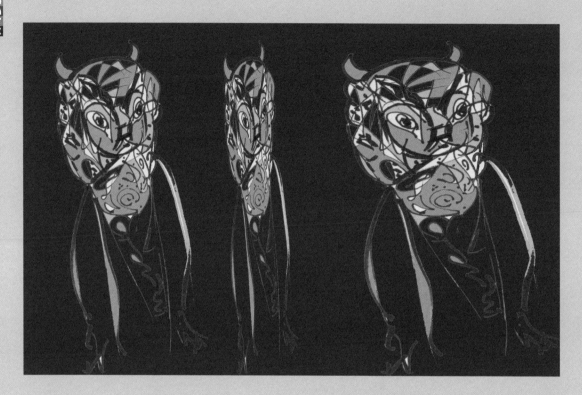

Jenny realized that the main reason she was afraid of people looking at her was because she imagined them all having the same set of eyes. It was invariably the merciless glare of Aunt Krezna. Krezna had smelled of rubbing alcohol and liked to dry (or bake) her hair by winding it into little knots on her scalp, coating the knots with olive oil, then inserting her head in the oven. She rested on her knees there, an effigy of suicide, praying for fifteen minutes until the egg timer dinged. Aunt Krezna could only wax enthusiastic about one subject, her Albanian homeland, which she had mistakenly left behind her. "Coming here was the biggest mistake of my life. Just as you were my sister's biggest, Jenny." If Jenny claimed to avoid punishment by saying that something she had done wrong was "an accident," Aunt Krezna would nod slowly and retort, "You like to say that because you were an accident." When Aunt Krezna had run through the obvious list of things to praise about Albania, she would enter the realm of "little known facts." Albania apparently had the fairest witchcraft trials in Europe until 1920.

Status update, 14 April 2013

Ellen treated him to a full inventory of the things in her life that she considered completely useless, keeping him in suspense till the last moment, when she rounded off the list (of course) with him.

Status update, 21 July 2009

His father never got his boat, and never even found the time to go sailing. But he did have that one day, at Willow's Point, when he sat in the waves with his son beside him talking about their future voyage, describing the adventures they would have together as a family to the last detail.

Status update, 17 June 2012

The braggadocio had leaked out of Victor's voice, he had let his hair grow long, and his shoes seldom matched anymore. It was time for a rousing pep talk from Cindy Skyloop, who always knew exactly the right thing to say. Her wonderful eyes always held a promise of toasted marshmallows. "Why would God have put you on this earth," she began, "if She didn't want you to sell insurance?"

Status update, 01 July 2010

The Woodster had been married five times, but this poor record was in fact misleading. His first wife, Rosalie, was a master of disguise and dialect and coital capers, and she had managed to fool him into marrying her over and over again. The fifth time he discovered her cunning ruse, he asked why, after so much misery, she couldn't let well enough alone? She shrugged. "I want you to admit I'm irreplaceable."

Status update, 18 December 2010

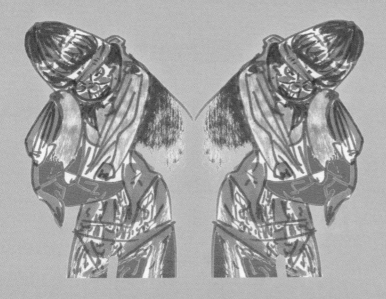

Chet was ugly, at least by the standards of the only world he knew. Perhaps if he'd been born on Saturn his looks would be just the thing. Like others so enigmatically ill-formed, he hid his dreams deeply. He never met a monster or beast in books that he couldn't identify with, and he craved beauty with the ardor of Quasimodo, Cyrano, and Frankenstein's creature, that towering mass of hurt made of corpsey odds and ends. Cyrano gave Chet hope, but finally he was an eavesdropper on happiness and the witty, romantic architect of a paradise that excluded him. The poet's soul is made for the shadowy wings, not center stage. His parents' principal objection to his appearance was that he didn't really harmonize with the mass of fine things in their home. Perhaps if they'd known a Surrealist, he could have designed a special chamber for him, with matching peculiarity. "No room for you," the elegant commodities in his home seemed to say. "We do our best to compensate for the disappointment you bring." He once overheard his mother tellling a friend, "At least we never spoiled him." Yes, they had kept him at arm's length from too much self-indulgence and frivolous joy. Chet somehow became friends with Maribelle, who loved his imagination, and said that she wished she had one just like it. He endeav-ored to have perfect communion with her spirit, and to grow a heart that she would admire. He knew, however, about the moat that separated her innermost castle from his yearning, crooked knight, and accepted the fact that she would remain a blessed vision of love rather than the real thing.

Status update, 11 June 2013

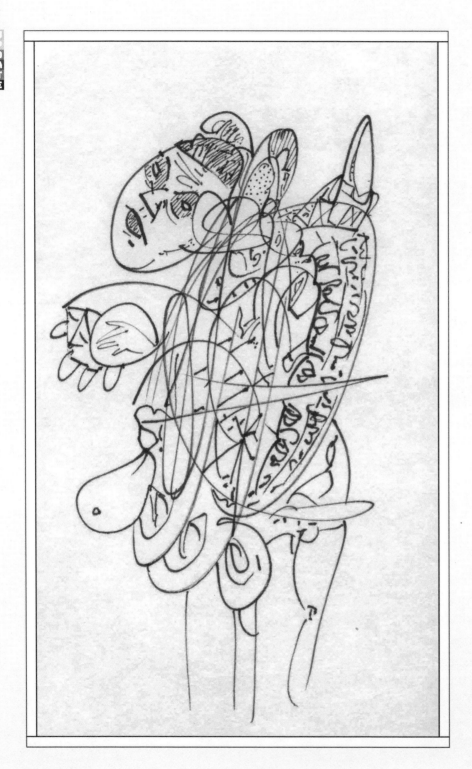

Once he had captured her imagination, he set about torturing it.

Status update, 04 September 2010

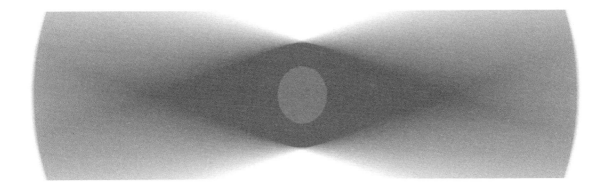

Dad had been out of the picture for a long time, and seemed uncharacteristically confused when he showed up. He wanted to be brought up to date, and "get oriented", as he put it. He didn't like to spend money in restaurants but he agreed to accompany me, if that was my routine. Once inside, he complimented the waitress profusely, called her "honey," and told her to bring him "whatever's good, whatever you want me to have. I'm not fussy." He asked me, in a slightly forced, offhand manner, about how his business was going as he watched me saw away at my pancake. "You could do with a bit more syrup," he said, and handed me the Log Cabin Maple, which he remembered. So many parts of the environment felt odd to him, but he wanted to appear on top of things. He still had his old need to be "with it" intact. He was humming "On a Clear Day, You Can See Forever," and tapping his foot under the table to keep time, while thinking his own thoughts. I didn't want to alarm him about the business or anyrhing else, so I said things were going fine. He seemed satisfied with that, and didn't press matters. He stirred uncomfortably in his chair, and tried to settle in. He may have had a hunch that his visit was a little tenuous, and that I could shoo him away at any moment because he was dead. He wasn't in a mood to declare his preferences with his usual gusto. Timidity didn't suit him at all, and I hoped he could find a topic that would allow him to hold forth with his effortless authority. He suddenly excused himself, food still untouched, and said he was going to the washroom. Two minutes later I saw him through the restaurant window slowly pedalling toward the post office on his old bicycle. I waved goodbye, but he didn't look back. How he hated emotional farewells.

Status update, 16 June 2013

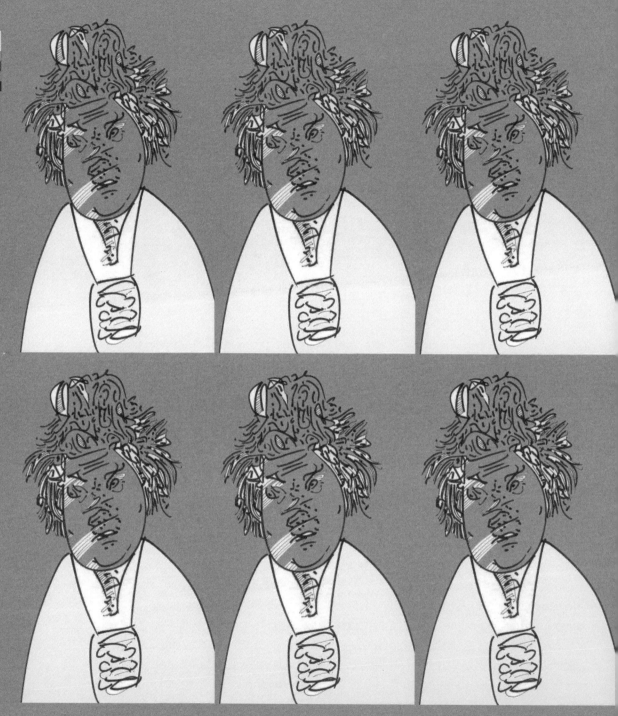

"How you underestimated me, Joan." He wiped the tears from her cheek.
"Nothing – nothing can destroy my illusions."

Status update, 28 April 2013

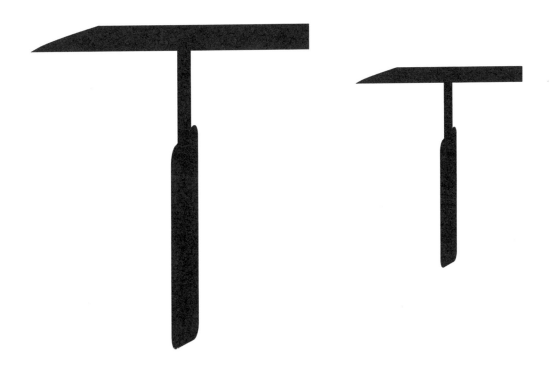

The wedding night was ruffled by some performance anxiety and unflattering truth telling on both sides. But Len and Angie soon had other fish to fry. Their attention was roused by the sounds of a scuffle just outside their door. Rufus Painter, an old flame of Angie's was lying in the hallway with an ice pick buried deep in his throat Had he spent his last moments on earth spying on them, Len wondered, suspiciously, and had Angie encouraged him to do so at the reception, for old times' sake? Angie thought about how different her life might be (perhaps better, who could say?) if it was Len instead of Rufus lying there with an icepick for an Adam's apple and Rufus calmly examining the corpse. The forensic side of Len wanted to examine the whole body of his former rival, but felt Angie might question his motives. Soon they did their best impression of raising a hue and cry. They were in the exciting first stage of a criminal investigation, when the search of every nook and cranny would be conducted, but in vain. Their wedding night, thank God, was salvaged by these new developments.

Status update, 18 March 2012

Alison remembered an occasion, not so very long ago, when her family was all gath-
ered together and there was a moment – an expanding instant – when she looked
from face to face and felt sure that they were all happy at the same time. She wished
for a powerful magician to appear at her doorstep who could let her see and feel
once more how she saw things then.

Status update, 24 December 2013

It was time for Karl to start over, and he knew just how to do it. He met an out-of-work childless couple who reminded him of his parents in the hopeful, pre-Karl days, only with more style, wit, and decency. He hired them to move in with him in the home he'd longed to live in as a child and give him a second upbringing. He drew up guidelines for EVERY situation. Then he auditioned a group of children in search of a prettier, caring sister and fun-loving friends who valued his leadership.

Status update, 19 September 2011

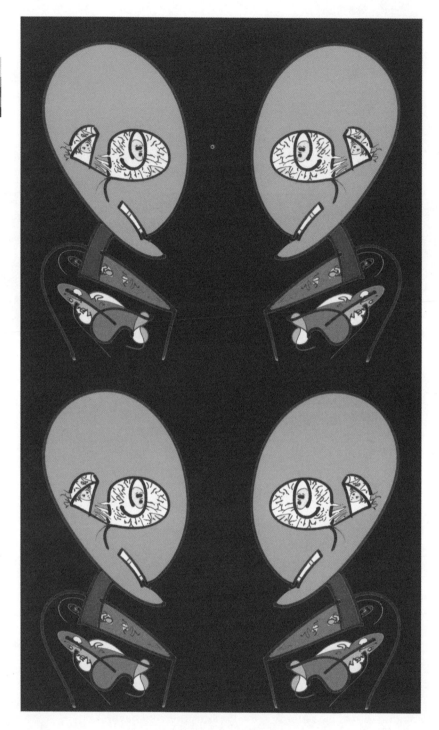

George bid a touching farewell to himself at the station.

Status update, 22 July 2009

George Toles

July 29, 2015 ·

To be misunderstood by someone you love is to feel like a child. To be humiliated or embarrassed is to feel like a child. To jump into a pool that's too cold is to feel like a child. And so it is for other things. To make mistakes, to not remember the answer, to have a joke fall flat, to toss and turn at night in fear, to lose one's way, to be caught up in a book, to roast marshmallows, to have gorged on food, to spy on a neighbour or co-worker. And, of course, to be dying is to feel like a child.

👍 You, Melissa Steele, Daniel Chen and 126 others   19 Comments 6 Shares

👍 Like   💬 Comment

ACKNOWLEDGMENTS

To my wife, Melissa Steele, who reads every update, my children, Sam, Thomas, and Rachel. Also, Pam Perkins for all of her help. To the many Facebook readers who---over the years--have offered encouragement and expressed the hope that a book such as this one might be created.

And a special thank you to Matt Joudrey of At Bay Press, the ideal publisher, whose excitement about the project from our first meeting made everything seem possible, and whose numerous invaluable suggestions about design and structure have given the book just the right form.

Photograph by Sarah Jo Kirsch, processing by Bill Eakin

Cliff Eyland was born in Halifax, Nova Scotia.

Eyland was a curator at the Technical University of Nova Scotia School of Architecture (Daltech) and freelanced for the Plug In Institute of Contemporary Art in Winnipeg. From 1995 to 2005, Eyland was vice-president of the board of Plug In. In 1998 he was hired as an associate professor of painting at the University of Manitoba School of Art and was also director of Gallery One One One, both positions he held until 2010.

Eyland was represented by Gurevich Fine Art in Winnipeg. His work is held at the University of Manitoba Archives & Special Collections. In 2020, his alma mater, Nova Scotia College of Art and Design, has set up the "Cliff Eyland Memorial Scholarship" for painting students and endowed by his family.

Photograph by Sherab Rabzyor Yolmo

George Toles is a Distinguished Professor of Film and Literature at the University of Manitoba.

He is the author of *A House Made of Light: Essays on the Art of Film,* Paul Thomas Anderson, and the forthcoming *Curtains of Light: Essays on the Metaphysics of Theatrical Space on Film.* He has been posting mini-narratives called Status Updates on Facebook every day since 2009. Two collections of these updates, with accompanying illustrations by artist collaborators, will be published in the next year.

George has written or co-written the screenplays for numerous feature films made by Canadian director, Guy Maddin. These include *Archangel, Careful, Twilight of the Ice Nymphs, The Saddest Music in the World, Brand Upon the Brain, My Winnipeg,* and *Keyhole.* He also wrote the story and original screenplay for Canada's first stop-motion animated feature film, *Edison and Leo.*

type in use

BUNGEE

Helvetica Neue

SF PRO DISPLAY

Beth Ellen